MAP OF THE
NEBRASKA DIVISION

CORRECTED TO JUNE 7, 1948

SCALE OF MILES

10 5 0   10   20   30   40   50

N.

—*Union Pacific*

J. C. Chitwood

Dec. 7th, 1964

Unionville, Indiana

Route #1.

SMOKE
ACROSS
THE
PRAIRIE

SMOKE ACROSS THE PRAIRIE

UNION PACIFIC

NEBRASKA DIVISION

Ehernberger and Gschwind

The "HARVERT HAULERS", an oil painting by the noted railroad artist and designer, Otto Kuhler.

ACKNOWLEDGMENTS

The authors wish to thank the many individuals who assisted in the preparation of this book. Among those who supplied photographs and offered valuable technical assistance we would like to give special thanks to John H. Conant, George Wm. Corben, Thomas O. Dutch, R. B. Grenard, Jr., Henry R. Griffiths, Jr., W. L. Haas, R. H. Kindig, W. W. Kratville, J. F. Larison, T. W. Mahoney, Otto C. Perry, Al Rose, Dick Rumbolz, Lou Schmitz, Arthur Stensvad, The Union Pacific Railroad, The Hastings Tribune, The Kearney Hub, and the Photo Center-Sidney, Nebraska. Our appreciation to Mr. E. C. Schafer, Director of Public Relations, Union Pacific Railroad and the members of his department for their assistance. The title page oil painting was graciously provided by Otto Kuhler. The cover illustration was drawn especially by Chapter Art Director Robert E. Jensen. The locomotive line drawings in the center of the book are from the pen of noted illustrator Joe Barros. Members of the Intermountain Chapter who aided in layout and editing include F. Hol Wagner, Jr., Stuart Sutton and William Marvel.

Library of Congress
No. 64-66031

Printed in the United States of America
by Bradford-Robinson Printing Co.
Denver, Colorado

Clouds of smoke and steam cascade into a threatening winter sky as Challengers 3804 and 3838 swing an eastbound freight around a gentle curve at Beck, Nebraska. December 1, 1956.—*A. E. Stensvad*

Published by
THE INTERMOUNTAIN CHAPTER,
NATIONAL RAILWAY HISTORICAL SOCIETY, INC.
P. O. Box 921, Golden, Colorado 80402

E. L. Pardee
National President

William C. Jones
Chapter President

Robert E. Wood
National Director

Kenneth C. Crist
Director of Publications

Robert E. Jensen
Art Director

Reminiscing about railroading on the Nebraska Division is solid satisfaction because this is where I got my start with Union Pacific.

Smoke Across the Prairie certainly brings to mind the men and machines it took to weld these segments into an operating part of the great railroad that is U. P.

The importance of steam power and its days on the Nebraska Division are well digested in this book.

A. E. Stoddard
President
Union Pacific Railroad

FOREWORD

For the greater part of a century, a traveler on the Great Plains, approaching the main line of the Union Pacific Railroad, across the length of the Nebraska Division, beheld in the distance a long finger of smoke haze, stretching across the prairie from horizon to horizon. This was his first visible evidence of the steam power of the mighty railroad, long before even the first faint sound of whistle or exhaust could reach his ear. The great canopy of smoke stretched along the Valley of the Platte and hung over Lodge Pole Creek as far as the eye could see. It reached westward from the banks of Mighty Missouri at Council Bluffs and Omaha; it swept above the fields of corn, and alfalfa, and sugar beets; it floated over rolling wheat fields and vast range lands dotted by countless herds of cattle; it pointed ever westward; and finally drifted over the Wyoming capitol at Cheyenne — — — to dissipate at last in the high, thin air of the uplands, at the foot of the Rockies. This awe-inspiring banner of smoke across the prairie was undoubtedly the most memorable trademark and symbol of the Nebraska Division of the Union Pacific, during the long era of steam locomotion.

To those who were fascinated by mountain railroading during the steam era (and who was not?) flatland railroading, on a prairie division, may have seemed, at first glance, dull and undramatic by comparison. But this was only an illusion! For while the prairie railroad may have lacked the sheer drama of the ceaseless battle between heavy power and steep grades, in a setting of breathless grandeur and majesty, it had its own share of spine-tingling action and romantic allure. For who could fail to be fascinated by the sight of a long freight train rolling rapidly across the vast sweep of plains, under an endless sky; or a fast passenger train cascading along at a fabulous clip toward a rendezvous with the Blue Pacific, behind a high-drivered black monster which voiced its exhilaration into the prairie winds. Nor was prairie railroading, as on the Nebraska Division, merely stereotyped by heavy power, great speed, or changeless stretches of straightaway track. For another world existed just over the hill, where the branch or secondary line wound its way along. The lover of quaintness, of individuality, and of the unexpected needed only to follow the less frequent plume of smoke which disappeared into the distance away from the main line, to find his desires fulfilled. For there he found light rails heading out into the more remote reaches of the prairie, often following an ever-diminishing stream, crossing and re-crossing it en route to a small terminus where rails ended in a setting straight out of yesterday. Ancient, diminutive locomotives, long since banished from the main line by progress, followed the light rails through a peaceful countryside, shattering the tranquility of the ubiquitous trackside cottonwood trees with their passage and raining down sparks and cinders on their unprotesting foliage.

This, then, was the Union Pacific's Nebraska Division during the great steam era. Why a publication devoted entirely to one such division? All too often, the mighty Overland Route is remembered, under steam, mainly for the thunder of heavy power up Sherman Hill, the roar of articulateds over the Wahsatch, or the rumble of heavy tonnage over the Sierra Nevada. In his haste to reach the scenic uplands of the West, the railroad fan-photographer sometimes overlooked what he may have considered the drab spectacle of railroading on the plains. In all fairness, he had more than a passing acquaintance with the

Nebraska Division but did he really know it in its entirety? Probably not, for while the sight of a mighty 4-12-2 heading westward out of Omaha, a 4-8-4 streaking down the Platte Valley near Kearney, or a huge 4-6-6-4 pounding along somewhere west of North Platte may all have been familiar to him, yet he probably missed much of the excitement of the Nebraska Division under steam. Few, indeed, were those who knew the Hastings Branch, for instance, when heavy power trudged across the apparently interminable Platte River bridge at Denman; or those who saw the 2-10-2's come charging into Beatrice, or Sterling. Fewer still were those who witnessed the picturesque spectacle of a light 2-8-0 wandering along the banks of the North Loup River, bound for Ord. Seldom, if ever, did the steam enthusiast avail himself of the opportunity to watch and photograph a sugar beet extra trailing along behind a clanking 2-8-2, virtually in the shadow of Scotts Bluff on the far reaches of the North Platte Cut-Off; and he doubtless missed forever the rare pleasure of framing in his camera view finder one of the tiniest of antique Consolidations as it rambled over one of the countless trestles on the Kearney Branch, seemingly far removed from the throbbing pulse of the main line.

This volume does not intend, however, to present an all-time pictorial review of steam power and operation on the division throughout the entire era of steam. Instead it attempts, in the main, to afford a last backward glance at the sunset years, for however sad they may have seemed to the lover of the steam locomotive, they were, nevertheless, among the most interesting years of all. For this was the age of contrasts! Displaced oil burners from the dieselized divisions of the Far West worked side by side with coal burners of long standing residence. It was an era which saw an 0-6-0 or a 2-8-0 of ancient vintage outlast huge articulateds and Northerns, less than a quarter of a century old.

It is our hope, then, that the following pages will recall smoke-filled memories and help to re-create a vanished era for those who knew it; and serve, at least to some small extent, to acquaint the unfamiliar with the Nebraska Division of a colorful and now departed age.

J. L. E.
F. G. G.
Callaway, Nebraska

In 1937 the U.P. Shops gave 4-6-2 #2906 (along with 4-8-2 #7002) a brown and yellow streamlined shroud for service on the "Forty Niner" inaugurated to serve San Francisco's 1939 Golden Gate Exposition.—*Union Pacific*.

Winter holds the Nebraska Division in its icy grip as Extra 9507 west charges out of Omaha in February of 1952.—*W. W. Kratville*

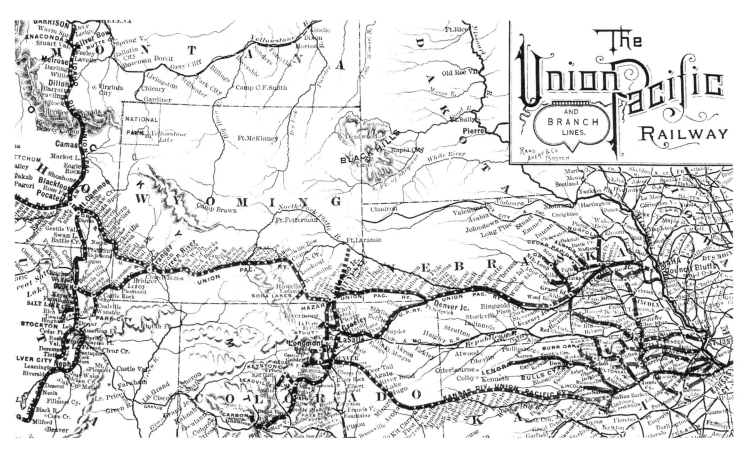

An early map of the Union Pacific shows a vastly abbreviated system compared to that of today, with much construction yet to come.—*Union Pacific*

MAIN LINE FIRST SUB-DIVISION
Council Bluffs, Iowa to North Platte, Nebraska

Rising from an elevation of approximately 1000 feet above sea level in the Missouri River bottomlands (983 feet at Council Bluffs........1033 at Omaha) the First Sub-Division of the Nebraska Division climbs to an elevation of 2802 feet at North Platte, 285 miles west of Council Bluffs. With the exception of the first 25 miles, the entire main line of the sub-division lies in the Platte River Valley, extending through one of the most fertile agricultural areas in the United States. The city of North Platte itself is located just west of the confluence of the North and South forks of the Platte, the main arterial waterway across Nebraska. Construction began on this segment of the Union Pacific in 1866, was completed in 1867, and double tracked to North Platte by 1910. In 1908, construction of a 12-mile section of new line just west of Omaha, known as the Lane Cut-Off, resulted in a saving of 9 miles and elimination of grades and curves of the circuitous older segment, now know as the Old Main Line.

Council Bluffs, Omaha, Grand Island and North Platte served as subdivision points and steam locomotive terminals and shops were maintained at these points during the steam era. Small engine houses were also located at Valley, Columbus and Kearney for servicing branch line and local power.

Because of easy grades, the First Sub-Division has always been the racetrack of the system, particularly for passenger and mail trains, and trains arriving late on this segment often left it "on time." High speed freight operation has always been routine, as well. The sight of a high-wheeled Pacific, sleek Northern, or powerful 4-12-2 galloping down the Platte Valley at break-neck speed, like a rail-borne Pegasus, was synomous with the age of steam on the First Sub-Division.

OLD MAIN LINE
Summit to Lane

While the construction of the Lane Cut-Off relegated the original main line to virtual branch line status, this segment, through South Omaha and along the Valley of Papillion Creek, bears little resemblance to the typical branch line of light, rusty rails and weed-grown right-of-way. Boasting double track for the more than six and one-half miles from Summit to Gilmore, the line is protected by the automatic block signals throughout its length. Considerable freight traffic moves across the Old Main Line, particurlarly livestock bound for the South Omaha stockyards, but scheduled passenger trains are only a fond memory of pre-1908 days.

BEATRICE BRANCH
Valley to Beatrice

The Beatrice Branch actually constitutes part of a bridge line between the main line and the Kansas Division. The branch, 96.8 miles in length, comprises approximately the northern half of a 189-mile north-south line, connecting with the Kansas City-Denver main line of the Kansas Division at Manhattan. At Marysville, 37.4 miles south of Beatrice, also on the Kansas Division, a connection is also made with the former St. Joseph & Grand Island Railroad, now part of the Union Pacific. Omaha-Kansas City freight service operates over the Beatrice Branch and via Marysville, Upland and Menoken, Kansas. The Beatrice Branch also connects with the Stromsburg Branch at Valparaiso. A four-stall engine house formerly housed steam power at Beatrice.

Originally a portion of Omaha & Republican Valley Railway, a Union Pacific subsidiary formed by the merger of a number of smaller independent lines, construction of the Beatrice Branch was completed in piecemeal fashion. The Valley to Lincoln portion was completed in 1877, while rails reached Beatrice from the south in 1881. The Lincoln-Beatrice segment was completed in 1884.

STROMSBURG BRANCH
Valparaiso to Central City

The Nebraska Division's lone east-west branch south of the Platte, the Stromsburg Branch, extends westward from Valparaiso, on the Beatrice Branch, for 75 miles to Central City on the main line, 22 miles east of Grand Island. Originally a portion of the Omaha & Republican Valley Railway network, construction of the line progressed during 1877-79, reaching Stromsburg during the latter year. Twenty-seven years later, in 1906, a 23-mile extension was completed to Central City, affording a direct outlet to the west, via the main line. Scheduled trains on the branch operate from Valley, on the main line, to Valparaiso, on the Beatrice Branch, then over the Stromsburg line to Central City and on to Grand Island, via the main line. Formerly, trains operated into Lincoln, on the east end, instead of to Valley.

NORFOLK BRANCH
Columbus to Norfolk

A trio of branch lines, to Norfolk, Albion, and Spalding, extend northwestward from Columbus, comprising part of a one-time U.P. subsidiary with the pretentious title of Omaha, Niobrara & Black Hills Railroad. Easternmost of these lines is the 50.4 mile Norfolk Branch, constructed in 1879. A connection is made at Norfolk with the CSTPM&O (Omaha Road) as well as with the Chicago & Northwestern. A 2-stall engine house formerly served steam power at that point.

ALBION BRANCH
Oconee to Albion

The 33.7 mile Albion Branch, constructed in 1880, extends westward through the Loup River Valley, from Oconee, on the Norfolk Branch, 9.4 miles north of Columbus, to Genoa. It then swings northwestward, along Beaver Creek, to its terminus at Albion. Although, as on many branch lines today, train service is infrequent, this branch once boasted a passenger train which operated on a through schedule between Albion and Omaha, via Oconee and Columbus and the main line.

CEDAR RAPIDS BRANCH
Genoa to Spalding

Listed officially on U.P. employees' timetables as the Cedar Rapids Branch, this 44.58 mile line is probably better known locally as the Spalding Branch. Westernmost of the three Columbus Branches, it extends from Genoa, junction point with the Albion Branch, to Spalding, 65 miles northwest of Columbus. The 30.3 mile segment from Genoa to Cedar Rapids was constructed in 1883-84. Cedar Rapids remained the terminus until 1902 when a 14-mile extension was added to Spalding. From Genoa to Fullerton the branch follows the broad Loup River Valley, then turns northwestward up the scenic Cedar River Valley to its terminal.

ORD BRANCH
Grand Island to Ord

Like Columbus, Grand Island boasted a three-pronged branch line network extending northwestward until 1947 when the Pleasanton Branch faded from existence. Longest of these branches is the 61-mile Ord Branch, which follows the Valley of the North Loup River for nearly two-thirds of its length, from St. Paul to Ord. Construction on the 22-mile segment from Grand Island to St. Paul was completed in 1880. In 1882, North Loup became the end of track when a 27-mile extension was added, and in 1886 the line was completed to Ord. Like several other Nebraska Division Branches, the Ord, Loup City, and Pleasanton lines were all a part of the once extensive Omaha & Republican Valley Railway, U. P.'s ubiquitous Nebraska subsidiary. An interesting feature of the Ord Branch is the 1.2 mile Scotia Spur, completed from Scotia Junction, 17.5 miles east of Ord, to the village of Scotia, in 1882. Scotia lies on the opposite side of the river from the branch, which necessitated a spur and trestle across the North Loup, to reach the town, on the east side of the river. A single-stall engine house at Ord once housed motive power during the steam era. A similar structure at St. Paul served steam power on the Loup City and Pleasanton branches.

LOUP CITY BRANCH
St. Paul to Loup City

Completed in 1885-86, the 39-mile Loup City Branch swings southwestward from St. Paul, along the Middle Loup Valley, then curves northwestward to Loup City, 61 miles from Grand Island, describing the shape of an inverted arc. Although it follows the river valley for its entire length, the line remains north of the Middle Loup River itself en route to its terminus. However, several small drainage streams are crossed, including one just east of Loup City with the unromantic name of Dead Horse Creek, which is hardly descriptive of the pleasant territory the branch traverses.

PLEASANTON BRANCH
Boelus to Pleasanton

The ill-fated Pleasanton Branch extended southwestward along the South Loup Valley from Boelus, on the Loup City Branch, 18.6 miles west of St. Paul, to Pleasanton, a distance of 22.42 miles, or nearly 63 miles overall, from Grand Island. Construction from Boelus to Nantasket, 10 miles, was completed in 1887 and rails reached Pleasanton in 1890. The line was apparently projected on up the South Loup Valley to Callaway and beyond, and some grading was completed between the two points but no rails were laid beyond Pleasanton. In 1947, declining revenues, coupled with a disastrous cloudburst and resultant flooding along the adjacent South Loup River which virtually obliterated the line, brought about its sudden and untimely end.

HASTINGS BRANCH
Gibbon to Hastings

Although konwn officially as the Hastings Branch, this line actually has main line status, affording a short cut from points west of Gibbon, on the main line, to the old St. Joseph & Grand Island trackage at Hastings and direct access to Kansas City via Marysville and Menoken, Kansas. Often referred to as the "Gibbon Cutoff," this line swings southeastward from the main line at Gibbon, 13 miles east of Kearney, and extends to Hastings, a distance of 28 miles. Constructed during 1913-14 as the Hastings & Northwestern Railroad, the line today serves as an important bridge line for freight service only. In other years, however, typical branch line service was given, in the form of a mixed train and a motor car in passenger service. The latter operated in con-

junction with similar service on the Kearney Branch, resulting in virtual Hastings-Kearney-Stapleton service for many years.

KEARNEY BRANCH
Kearney to Stapleton

The 102-mile Kearney Branch, formerly known as the Callaway Branch, began life in 1890 as the Kearney & Black Hills Railway, when the 65-mile segment from Kearney to Callaway was completed. Absorption of this subsidiary by the parent U. P. took place within a few years and while the line never realized the ambitions of its original title, a 37-mile extension to Stapleton was completed in 1912. The branch was projected westward beyond Stapleton, with some grading completed, but no rails were ever laid beyond this terminus. From the main line at Kearney, the Stapleton Branch, as it is known locally, heads northwestward along the Wood River Valley to its head, a few miles east of Callaway, then descends into the South Loup River Valley, which it follows the remainder of the distance to Stapleton. Because of many crossings of the Wood and South Loup Rivers and their tributaries, the line averages nearly one trestle per mile of track. Another interesting feature of the branch is the fact that westbound trains actually leave Kearney heading due east, as the line swings around the east edge of the city in a long, continuous curve until a northwesterly direction is attained. Union Pacific's first McKeen motor car inaugurated motorized passenger service on the system when it was placed in operation on this line in 1905. In 1955, a half century after Mr. McKeen's marvel started it all, the final run by a passenger motor car on the Nebraska Division was completed on this branch. A two-stall engine house at Stapleton, originally located in Callaway, served motive power on the branch until the close of steam operation.

MAIN LINE   SECOND SUB-DIVISION
North Platte, Nebraska to Cheyenne, Wyoming

Extending for 225 miles across western Nebraska and southeastern Wyoming, the Second Sub-Division of the Nebraska Division follows the Valley of the South Platte River from North Platte, Nebraska to Julesburg, Colorado, where the line cuts across the extreme northeastern corner of that state. It then follows the Lodge Pole Creek Valley back into the Nebraska Panhandle and on into Wyoming, crossing the high plains of eastern Wyoming and dropping down Archer Hill the final miles into Cheyenne, where the Nebraska Division officially terminates at the east yard limits. The rails climb unspectacularly, but steadily, from an elevation of 2802 feet at

North Platte, to 6060 feet at Cheyenne, nearly 875 feet higher than the "mile-high city" of Denver, Colorado. The landscape changes steadily, from the fertile bottomlands of the Platte to wide plains interspersed by occasional rocky bluffs, and reaches its grand climax with the final sweep of the Great Plains to the foothills of the Rockies, with the Snowy Range towering in the southwest.

Track construction between North Platte and Cheyenne was completed in 1867 and the final segment of second track was opened to traffic in 1917. Extensive roundhouse facilities at both terminals, as well as a smaller structure at Sidney, housed and serviced steam locomotives, and at one time steam locomotive shops were also located at all three points.

Perhaps no other type of power symbolized the final valiant years of steam on this section of the main line more than the heavy Challengers, and the pulse-quickening sight of a 3900 thundering westward into the sunset provided an indestructible memory for anyone familiar with the Second Sub-Division during that momentous era.

NORTH PLATTE BRANCH
O'Fallons to Gering

Longest of all Nebraska Division branches, the 146-mile North Platte Branch was completed to Gering in 1911. Construction, which began in 1907, reached Lutherville by the end of that year; Oshkosh in 1908; and Northport in 1909, 114 miles from O'Fallons. Northport, where an interchange with the Burlington Route is maintained, was destined to remain the terminus of the branch until 1911 when the final segment to Gering was completed. In 1939, approximately 33 miles of line were relocated between mileposts 24 and 57 because of the construction of the huge Kingsley Dam on the North Platte River and the resulting lake (McConaughy), which inundated much of the original right of way on this segment. Leaving the main line at O'Fallons, a rural siding 16.5 miles west of North Platte, the line extends up the North Platte Valley in a northwesterly direction for virtually its entire length. At Gering, a five-stall engine house served the variety of steam power which saw service on this branch through the years.

NORTH PLATTE CUT-OFF
Gering, Nebraska to South Torrington, Wyoming
and
Yoder, Wyoming to Egbert, Wyoming

The North Platte Cut-Off actually consists of a 54.7 mile extension of the Gering Branch, up the North Platte Valley to South Torrington, Wyoming and a 62.7 mile north-south line from Yoder, Wyoming, 35.7 miles west of Gering, to Egbert, on the main line, 32 miles east of Cheyenne. The name of this line is derived from the fact that it offers a short cut or cut-off from the upper end of the North Platte Branch to the main line, eliminating the necessity of routing all shipments the long way around, via O'Fallons. The Gering-South Torrington segment was constructed at various intervals, beginning in 1913, with completion taking place in 1926. The Yoder-Egbert section was completed in 1928, the last extensive railroad construction on the Nebraska Division. A two-stall engine house at South Torrington served steam power operating to that end of the line. Derailments or track damage on the main line between Cheyenne and North Platte sometimes results in re-routing main line traffic over the North Platte Cut-Off and North Platte Branch, due to heavy steel and good roadbed on these lines.

GERING BRANCH
Gering to Riford

The 9.8-mile Gering Branch, extending southward from Gering to Riford, reaches into the broad valley south of the North Platte River to tap a large sugar beet producing area. Beets are moved from "dumps" on this branch to a sugar refinery at Gering. Livestock loading pens are also located along the line but this branch sees little service except during the Fall season. This branch was constructed in 1927.

LYMAN BRANCH
Lyman to Stegall

The Lyman Branch, like the Gering Branch, serves mainly as an outlet to tap the sugar beet and livestock producing areas south of the North Platte River. Constructed in 1926-27, this line extends from Lyman, 22 miles west of Gering, to Stegall, 6.4 miles to the southeast.

SEARS BRANCH
Sears to Janise

Extending from a junction with the Lyman Branch at Sears, 2.8 miles south of Lyman, the Sears Branch extends an additional 2.8 miles southward to Janise. Like the Lyman and Gering Branches, this line exists mainly for the purpose of tapping the sugar beet growing areas south of the North Platte River. As on the other two branches, livestock loading pens are also located along the line. This branch was constructed in 1927.

THIRD SUB-DIVISION
Julesburg, Colorado to La Salle, Colorado

Leaving the main line of the Union Pacific at Julesburg, Colorado, 365 miles west of Council Bluffs, the Third Sub-Division of the Nebraska Division extends southwestward for 151 miles to La Salle, Colorado, where a junction is made with the Wyoming Division's Cheyenne-Denver line. Constructed in 1882 by the Colorado Central Railroad, a U. P. subsidiary, this sub-division was once a part of the old Colorado Division. The line serves as a short cut from Council Bluffs to Denver for the U.P., as prior to its construction, Council Bluffs-Denver traffic was routed via Cheyenne. A ten-stall engine house at Sterling and a four-stall structure at LaSalle stabled the iron horses in service on the Third Sub-Division. Although various types of steam power operated over this segment, probably none was more familiar during the latter decades of steam than the 2-10-2 type, and the usually uncelebrated 5000's performed faithfully between Julesburg and La Salle until replaced by dieselization.

Early day railroading on Nebraska Division branches was typified by 4-4-0 574 with a passenger local at Genoa, Nebraska, in 1894 (top) and Ten-wheeler 1010 (bottom), posing with her proud crew at Stromsburg, Nebraska, in 1899.—*Both Union Pacific*

The year and the engine number are the same as light 2-8-2 1938 switches a cut of cars at Council Bluffs, Iowa, on May 29, 1938.—*R. H. Kindig*

A pair of 2-10-2's, the 5050 and 5031, doublehead a westbound drag out of Council Bluffs on Independence Day, 1953.—*R. H. Kindig*

9514 lifts a black plume over the Missouri Valley as she heads west out of Council Bluffs with a 98-car extra on July 4, 1953.—*R. H. Kindig*

The 5057, a 2-10-2, and the 826, a 4-8-4, team up on a 54-car westbound freight out of Omaha on July 4, 1953.—*R. H. Kindig*

2-10-2's in tandem, 5057 and 5073, put their collective twenty drivers to the task of pulling a westbound extra out of the Omaha yards (top) while Northern 833 (bottom), in pre-smoke-lifter days, does the honors with the westbound Gold Coast leaving Omaha on March 25, 1949.—Top, *T. O. Dutch;* Bottom, *W. W. Kratville*

Framed by the familiar Nebraska cottonwoods, the 842 leads a westbound extra across a bridge on the Lane Cut-off west of Omaha. August 5, 1956. — *A. E. Stensvad*

7033, a 4-8-2, wheels westward near Summit, Nebraska, on August 31, 1952.—*R. H. Kindig*

A rare visitor to the east end of the division was Challenger 3949 passing eastward through Elkhorn, Nebraska, on a frosty Christmas Day, 1951. 3900's were seldom seen east of North Platte.—*W. W. Kratville*

No stranger, however, was the 9026 shaking the earth with her three-cylindered exhaust as she stamped away from the coal chute at Valley, Nebraska, heading east on September 14, 1955.—*J. L. Ehernberger*

Train No. 73, headed by the 9055, leaves the main line at Valley, follows Beatrice Branch steel past the well-filled engine house, and heads for Topeka, Kansas.—*J. H. Conant*

Veteran Oregon Short Line 2-8-2 No. 2557 teams with a 4-12-2 for the hard climb up Touhy Hill, on the Beatrice Branch.—*R. Rumbolz*

Consolidation 494, running late with Train No. 75, is passed by Motor Train 547, powered by the M-41, at Central City, Nebraska. Both trains are leaving the Stromsburg Branch at this point and are Grand Island bound, via the main line. June 7, 1947.—*J. H. Conant*

Wintry skies overhang Genoa, Nebraska, as Consolidation 489 heads out of town with the Albion Branch mixed. December 15, 1956.—*J. L. Ehernberger*

A few minutes after the Albion train has left, the 430 swings her short train for Spalding onto the Cedar Rapids Branch. Note the Albion Branch at left, background. Genoa, December 15, 1956.—*J. L. Ehernberger*

Train time at Cedar Rapids, Nebraska. Engine 430 arrives with No. 80, eastbound, on October 27, 1956.
—*J. L. Ehernberger*

The veteran 414 pauses at Dannebrog, Nebraska, on the Loup City Branch, with No. 288. As Nos. 85-86, this train has also completed a round trip on the short Pleasanton Branch.—*J. H. Conant*

Like a ghost from the past, Engine 428 returns, in October of 1958, for a few trips in branch line service. She follows the placid North Loup River near Scotia, Nebraska, on the Ord Branch (top, and left) and passes the inevitable cottonwoods and ripened corn near Elba (bottom), in a scene typical of Nebraska Division branches during the steam age. —*All, F. G. Gschwind*

The Hastings Branch under steam is recalled in these rare photographs. An eastbound extra headed by a 4-12-2 crosses the long Platte River trestle at Denman (top). In a scene once commonplace but now vanished from American railroading, the 9042 (left) takes on coal at Hastings on September 18, 1949 while a pair of 2-10-2's (bottom) meet at Hayland. Extra 5029 east roars up the hill while the westbound 5036 waits "in the hole."
—All, J. H. Conant

Extra 5069 west holds the passing track at Lexington, Nebraska, as 4-8-2 type No. 7000 surges past on the westbound main with the 2nd section of Train No. 7.—*J. L. Ehernberger Collection.*

A winter sunset lengthens shadows across the prairie as Consolidation 460 scurries across the South Loup River trestle near Finchville, Nebraska, on the upper reaches of the Kearney Branch, with an eastbound caboose hop. January 9, 1955.—*F. G. Gschwind*

The elder statesman of Union Pacific 2-8-0's, jaunty little 105, crosses the meadows west of Callaway, Nebraska, on July 6, 1950 with Train No. 518. The run was normally made by a gas-electric motor car but a last-minute breakdown resulted in the use of the non-luxury equipment shown here.—*F. G. Gschwind*

The diminutive 113 steams impatiently at Stapleton, Nebraska, on December 9, 1948, awaiting the highball which will send her on her 102-mile journey down the branch to Kearney.—*J. L. Ehernberger Collection*

Livestock extras, like the 21-car Extra 407 east heading upgrade east of Callaway on October 17, 1954 were once familiar sights each autumn on Nebraska Division branches.—*F. G. Gschwind*

The first traces of a brewing thunderstorm appear in the western sky as 433 jogs eastward with No. 96 near Lodi, Nebraska, on a warm summer afternoon, July 18, 1954.—*F. G. Gschwind*

A valiant warrior of the high iron, No. 9000 thunders westward through Kearney on November 12, 1954 in a scene which arouses nostalgia for the three decades when 4-12-2's held sway on the Nebraska Division.—*F. G. Gschwind*

The weather is very warm but no more so than the U. P. main line at Kearney, Nebraska, on August 8, 1947 as Extra 5052 west rolls through town while an eastbound waits in the clear. Still another headlight appears beneath the coal chute in the distant background.—*J. L. Ehernberger Collection*

Heading west into the bright sunlight of late autumn, Northern 830 leaves Kearney with the second section of No. 5, the California Fast Mail, on November 12, 1954.—*F. G. Gschwind*

Stirring action transpires as extras pass on the prairie east of North Platte, Nebraska, on November 28, 1941. The westbound extra is headed by Mikado 2314 and, as Pearl Harbor is only a few days away, "Mikado" will soon be replaced by "MacArthur" as the designation for 2-8-2's.—*A. E. Stensvad*

Crowned by a plume of heavy black oil smoke, 3832 scorches the ballast west of Gothenburg, Nebraska, with a westbound hotshot on September 7, 1957. — *J. L. Ehernberger*

The first snowfall blankets the prairie as bald-faced 4-12-2 No. 9012 heads eastward from North Platte on December 4, 1953.—*A. E. Stensvad*

Lowly, unglamorous, but indispensable, is the local freight of the main line. Here a westbound "peddler" arrives in North Platte on January 22, 1954 behind the 2558.—*A. E. Stensvad*

A January thaw has reduced the snow to scattered patches as Extra 9028 west arrives at North Platte. January 13, 1954.—*A. E. Stensvad*

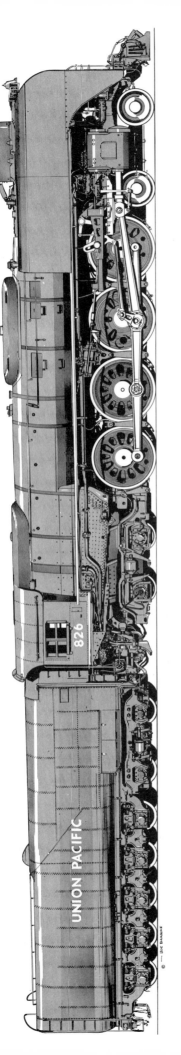

UNION PACIFIC NORTHERN (4-8-4) FOR DUAL SERVICE

Series	820-834
Cylinders, diameter and stroke	25x32 in.
Driving wheel diameter	80 in.
Boiler pressure	300 lbs. per sq. in.
Grate area	100.2 sq. ft.
Evaporative heating surface	4470 sq. ft.
Superheater heating surface	1900 sq. ft.
Weight on drivers	270,000 lbs.
Weight on lead truck	94,000 lbs.
Weight on trailing truck	119,000 lbs.
Weight of total engine	442,000 lbs.
Weight of tender (loaded)	406,500 lbs.
Tender capacity	25 tons; 23,500 gal.
Tractive force, engine	63,800 lbs.
Builder, date	Alco, 1939

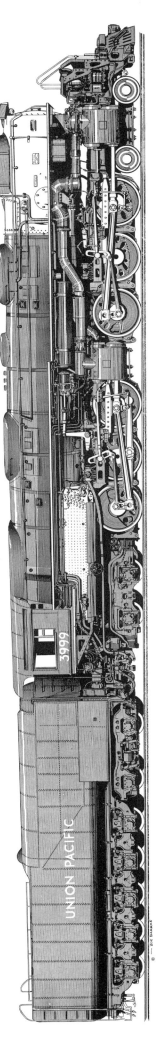

UNION PACIFIC CHALLENGER (4-6-6-4) FOR FREIGHT SERVICE

Series	3975-3999
Cylinders, diameter and stroke	21x32 in.
Driving wheel diameter	69 in.
Boiler pressure	280 lbs. per sq. in.
Grate area	132 sq. ft.
Evaporative heating surface	4817 sq. ft.
Superheater heating surface	2085 sq. ft.
Weight on drivers	407,500 lbs.
Weight on lead truck	102,000 lbs.
Weight on trailing truck	124,000 lbs.
Weight of total engine	633,500 lbs.
Weight of tender (loaded)	436,500 lbs.
Tender capacity	28 tons; 25,000 gals.
Tractive force, engine	97,350 lbs.
Builder, date	Alco, 1943

Joe Barros

In a magnificent panorama of smoke, steam, and steel, heavy Challenger 3992 casts a Vesuvius-like eruption into the skies of eastern Wyoming as she storms westward near Archer on August 17, 1957.—*J. L. Ehernberger*

9013 hurries a string of refrigerator cars out of town, past the telegraph operator's shanty and an eastbound extra waiting to enter the yards at West North Platte. September 26, 1953.—*A. E. Stensvad*

3941, a heavy 4-6-6-4, leaves a trail of smoke across the prairie west of North Platte as she rambles along, eastbound, near Birdwood, Nebraska, on November 24, 1956.—*A. E. Stensvad*

The 2256, one of a large fleet of work-horse 2-8-2's, handles a typical assignment as she rolls eastward near Brule, Nebraska, on Memorial Day, 1938, with local freight No. 242, unencumbered by heavy tonnage.—*R. H. Kindig*

2510 leads the westbound North Platte Branch local, No. 97, at West North Platte, July 30, 1954. At O'Fallons the train will leave the main line and swing onto the rails of the branch.—*A. E. Stensvad*

Near Broadwater, Nebraska, Train 98 heads eastward down the branch behind still another Mike, the 2309. June 29, 1954.—*A. E. Stensvad*

Fifty-year-old 418 waits at Lyman, Nebraska, near the Wyoming border, with Train 60, en route from South Torrington, Wyoming, to Gering, Nebraska, on June 12, 1950.—*A. E. Stensvad*

Scotts Bluff, famous landmark of the old Oregon Trail, maintains its eternal vigil over the plains as Extra 2206 west steams past the east switch at Costin, Nebraska, on October 8, 1957.—*J. L. Ehernberger*

Consolidation 733, bumped by diesels from home territory in the Pacific Northwest, chugs past the hay meadows at South Mitchell, Nebraska, and trails her exhaust into the crisp air of autumn. October 26, 1957.—*J. L. Ehernberger*

Engine 768 leaves Yoder, Wyoming, in 1956 with No. 59, the westbound "top-end" local, so named because of its operation on the upper end of the North Platte Cut-off.—*J. L. Ehernberger*

Mountain type 7862 climbs through evergreen-dotted hills near Albin-Tremain Tunnel with Mixed 353, en route from Yoder to Cheyenne. February, 1956.—*J. L. Ehernberger*

An unusual caboose hop, featuring the doubleheading 400 and 402, waits at Albin, Wyoming, on May 22, 1954.—*J. L. Ehernberger*

No. 353 arrives at Egbert, Wyoming, from Yoder behind the 7862, and will complete the remainder of her 95-mile journey to Cheyenne on main line trackage. 1956.—*J. L. Ehernberger*

Light Pacific 2809 churns her 77-inch drivers at a rapid clip as she rushes past the camera with No. 53, somewhere west of Egbert, Wyoming (top). At the time this rare photograph was taken, probably in the early 1930's, Trains 53-54 operated between North Platte and Cheyenne via the main line, the North Platte Branch, and the North Platte Cut-off.—*O. C. Perry*

No. 3832 trails a string of orange and yellow reefers around the curve at Point of Rocks near Sidney, Nebraska, on October 14, 1956.—*A. E. Stensvad*

Challengers meet at Julesburg, Colorado, August 30, 1955. The 3957, having refueled, pulls away from the coal chute with her eastbound train, but the oil-burning 3835 will roll on through this important junction. —*A. E. Stensvad*

The majesty and brute strength of Union Pacific's magnificent 4-12-2's was never portrayed more vividly than in these two views of 9040 westbound near Archer, Wyoming (left) and arriving at Cheyenne (right) on September 4, 1955.—*Both J. L. Ehernberger*

Mountain type 7853 leaves a trail of billowing smoke and steam behind No. 354 near Archer in a classic scene of steam railroading in winter—*All, J. L. Ehernberg*

Her engineer waves a greeting as the 2206 leads No. 354 around a curve near Archer on October 25, 1956.

Extra 9505 west, pounds around a curve at Pine Bluffs, Wyoming, with a portion of the landmark for which the town was named appearing in the right background.

With her 80-inch drivers pounding the steel of the Third Sub-Division, 4-8-4 No. 826 roars eastward down the South Platte Valley near Kuner, Colorado, on November 17, 1955.—*J. L. Ehernberger*

The 3700's were the last steam locomotives in regular service on the Nebraska Division and the 3715 and 3712 leaving Cheyenne on July 19, 1959 are symbolic of the close of an era.—*J. L. Ehernberger*

A classic example of passenger power of the past on the Nebraska Division was high-drivered Atlantic 10 (later renumbered 3309). Built to Harriman standards, 4-4-2's like her handled top assignments until advent of the 4-6-2's. All engines of this class were gone by 1934.—*W. L. Haas Collection*

STEAM MOTIVE POWER
ON THE NEBRASKA DIVISION

Steam power which appeared on the Nebraska Division through the years covered virtually all types and wheel arrangements on the Union Pacific System, from 4-4-0's through 4-8-8-4's. The greatest variety of power in service at one time was probably in evidence during the last twenty-five years of steam. By that time, many of the standbys of an earlier age, including the 4-4-0's, 4-6-0's, 4-4-2's and older classes of 0-6-0's were gone from the roster, and inroads had been made into the ranks of certain other types, including some Consolidations and light Pacifics. Standard freight power by that time (the mid-1930's) included 2-8-2's of the 2200-2300 series, 2-10-2's of the 5000 series, and those incomparable three-cylindered 4-12-2's, the 9000's, then rounding out their first decade of stellar service. Passenger service was capably handled by heavy Pacifics of the 2860-2911 series and by the 7000 class 4-8-2's. Light Harriman Pacifics of the 2800 series were still around in dwindling numbers, but their long tenure in passenger service was virtually over and they were assigned mainly to local freight or extra service and an occasional trip up the North Platte Branch. Switching assignments were handled by a wide

variety of power, including conventional 0-6-0's of the 4400 series; a very few United States Railway Administration 0-6-0's (4600's) of World War I days, mainly in service on the east end of the division; 2-8-0's of the 200-300 series, which also saw considerable action in local freight service; and some 1900 class 2-8-2's, which also doubled in local freight service. Not to be forgotten was the lone 0-8-0 on the roster, numbered 4500 and rebuilt from Consolidation 416, which spent most of her final years at Grand Island. Branch line duties were nearly 100% in the charge of the light 2-8-0's by this time, with the extinction of the 4-4-0's and the departure of the last two ten-wheelers, 1242 and 1243, for service on the Wyoming Division's Encampment Branch. The "fabulous 400's" were in branch line service throughout the division; one notable exception being the Kearney Branch where smaller Consolidations 105, 113 and 117, the last of their class, were still in command, due to light rail between Kearney and Callaway. In addition to branch line assignments the versatile 400's also performed capably in yard service and made appearances in main line local freight service as well. On the North Platte Branch 2-8-2's and 4-6-2's saw considerable service. On rare occasions, on the main line, a 2-8-8-0 would work as far east as Sidney.

In 1936 and 1937 two new types of steam power appeared on the system, the 4-6-6-4's and the 4-8-4's. The former, numbered in the 3900 series (later to be renumbered 3800's) were assigned to western divisions while the 4-8-4's, carrying the 800 number series, began taking over passenger duties, with an additional group of this type arriving in 1939.

After the outbreak of World War II, additional, heavier 4-6-6-4's were placed in service from 1942 through 1944, but in 1941 steam motive power history was made with the arrival of the titanic 4-8-8-4's, numbered in the 4000 series, with an additional group arriving in 1944. In that same year the final block of 4-8-4's was also added to the roster. The heavy articulateds followed their predecessors to western assignments while the dual-service 4-8-4's continued to predominate in passenger chores, although new diesel passenger units had already broken steam's complete domination in that service some years earlier. The first diesel switch engine arrived in late 1939 and the arrival of additional units the following year began the relentless trend of replacing steam power in yard service. With the elimination of the old Colorado Division and its absorption into the Wyoming, Kansas and Nebraska Divisions, the Julesburg-La Salle line became a part of the Nebraska Division and with it came the 2400 series USRA 2-8-2's which had been a part of the scene there for some years.

With the cessation of hostilities, the U. P. embarked on an accelerated scrapping program which swiftly began to remove many veterans from the roster. Diesels began arriving on the system in force, although most of the early freight units were sent west, where total dieselization of several divisions was being carried out. This resulted in considerable steam power from these divisions being shunted eastward, and as a result, strangers from the west began to appear on the Nebraska Division. From the Oregon Short Line came 2-8-2's of the 2000 and 2500 series; 5300 series 2-10-2's; 9500 series 4-12-2's; and a handful of 2-8-0's of the 500-600 series. From the Oregon-Washington Railroad and Navigation Company lines of U. P. came a few 700 series 2-8-0's; 2100 series 2-8-2's; and a few heavy Pacifics of the 3218 class. From the Los Angeles and Salt Lake segment of the system, but via other divisions to which they had previously been exiled by dieselization, came 2700 series 2-8-2's; 5500 series 2-10-2's; 7850 class 4-8-2's; and a few of the rare 5090 series 4-10-2's, formerly 3-cylindered engines before rebuilding. A lone LA&SL 2-8-0, the 6035, arrived in 1955, possibly for branch line service but a broken frame suffered en route, prevented her from ever turning a driver under her own power on the Nebraska Division. Coal strikes during this period often resulted in unusual motive power assignments

for brief periods, and under these conditions the gargantuan 4-8-8-4's made rare, brief appearances as far east as North Platte. Heavy 4-6-6-4's were now in service west of North Platte, putting in an occasional appearance at the Council Bluffs roundhouse, as well.

As the second half of the Twentieth Century dawned and it was obvious that steam power was making its last stand, some final changes were taking place. By this time the 4-8-4's had assumed the other half of their dual-service role, and although diesels had bumped them from virtually all passenger assignments, they were turning in equally brilliant performances in freight service, even though maintenance of steam power was by now at a minimum. Gone, by this time, were the Pacifics; the 0-6-0's had nearly disappeared; and the 2-8-0's 2-8-2's, 4-6-2's and 2-10-2's, as well as the few 4-10-2's, were stored in long lines which were becoming shorter day by day. Almost inconceivably, even the seemingly invincible 4-12-2's were now beginning to succumb to the cutter's torch. Yet there were anachronisms! The 400 class Consolidations were still holding down branch line assignments, including the Kearney Branch, where installation of heavier steel had brought an end to the reign of the jaunty little 100's. The 4-6-6-4's were swiftly becoming the "standard" steam power in freight service on the main line of the division; with the older 3800 series oil-burning Challengers in service between Council Bluffs and Cheyenne and both coal-burning 3900's and oil-burning 3700's pounding the tall steel between North Platte and Cheyenne.

By 1955 the roof was caving in for steam all along the division with one point after another falling to the continued inroads of the diesel. Wheel arrangements still remaining to the roster could be counted on the fingers of one hand. Diesels had taken over on most branch lines, though rush seasons brought out 400's again, but in swiftly thinning ranks. Yet as late as 1955, one of the ancient 2-8-0's made an appearance on the main line on a weed spraying train. The remaining main line freight assignments still handled by steam power were going to the still-classy Northerns and Challengers but each season saw fewer steamers returning to service, and for shorter periods of time. In the Fall of 1958 a sudden upsurge of traffic brought out the 4-8-4's and 4-6-6-4's again, but for the 800's it was their final curtain call. Almost unbelievably, however, switcher 4466 reappeared briefly in yard service at Grand Island while Consolidation 428 worked the Loup City and Ord Branches for a few memorable days, as time seemed to turn backward for the moment.

Finally, 1959 became the year of Armageddon for Nebraska Division steam power — the last battles being fought by 3700 series Challengers between

North Platte and Cheyenne for a brief period that summer. There would be a few postscripts — one Challenger remained in snow melter service, but under a cumbersome number assigned to maintenance of way equipment. Northern 844, renumbered 8444 to make way for a new diesel carrying her former number, almost sacrilegiously, remained on the active roster, reliving her glorious past on occasional excursions, but with an uncertain future.

A few other steam veterans were placed on permanent display at various points across the division, to serve as silent but tangible reminders of a bygone day. So as the last active articulated clanked to a final stop, that summer of 1959, the curtain fell forever on a long and colorful era and all that remained was for the scrappers at Council Bluffs, Omaha, Grand Island, North Platte and Cheyenne to complete their final job.

105 at Callaway, Nebraska, July 13, 1947 was originally a Baldwin camelback of 1887, rebuilt to conventional type in 1894, and was the last survivor of her class.—*F. G. Gschwind*

A considerably heavier 2-8-0 was the 238. Valley, Nebraska, August, 1945.— *J. L. Ehernberger Collection*

300's, except 350-58 which were ex-Southern Pacific, were an extension of the 200 series. 332 is at Lincoln, Nebraska, September 6, 1954. Vanderbilt and rectangular tenders were frequently interchanged.—*J. L. Ehernberger Collection*

414 at Callaway, March 30, 1955. 400's were almost universal branch line power on the division for years and also saw considerable switching and main line local service.—*F. G. Gschwind*

561, at Grand Island on August 8, 1954, came from the Oregon Short Line and may have been the only 500 to see service on the Nebraska Division. — *J. H. Conant*

603, at Lincoln, October 23, 1954, was also ex-OSL. The 500-600 series saw only limited service on the division.— *J. L. Ehernberger Collection*

Oil-burning 748 at South Torrington, Wyoming, on November 14, 1954. Originally OWRR&N power, 700's came from the Kansas Division after diesels took over there; were used mainly in the Gering area on the North Platte Branch and Cut-off.—*J. L. Ehernberger*

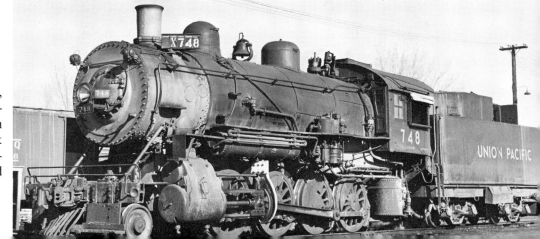

808 at North Platte, Nebraska, January 28, 1946 in pre-smoke lifter days. 4-8-4's may well have been the finest UP power of all time.—*F. G. Gschwind*

Heavier 830 at Kearney, Nebraska, November 12, 1954 shows evidence of changes and improvements over first series.—*F. G. Gschwind*

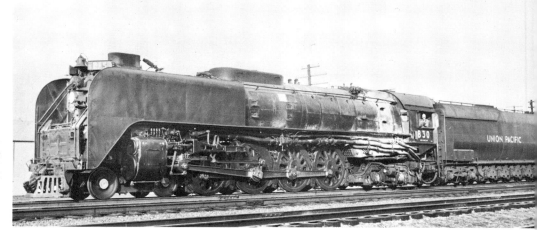

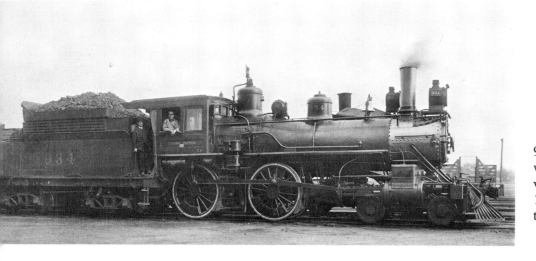

934 at Spalding, Nebraska, about 1920, was typical of rebuilt 4-4-0's which survived on the division until the early 1930's, running out their last miles on the branches.—*Union Pacific*

Venerable Ten-wheeler 1243, at Columbus, Nebraska, about 1924, saw considerable service on various division branches and was one of the last two 4-6-0's on the system, along with sister 1242. She went to the Wyoming Division in the early 1930's, received a Vanderbilt tender and smaller drivers and is still being held from the scrap pile, pending future disposition.—*Union Pacific*.

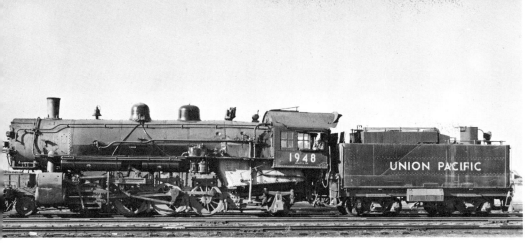

2-8-2 No. 1948 at North Platte, April 8, 1948. 1900's saw considerable yard work as well as local service.—*F. G. Gschwind*

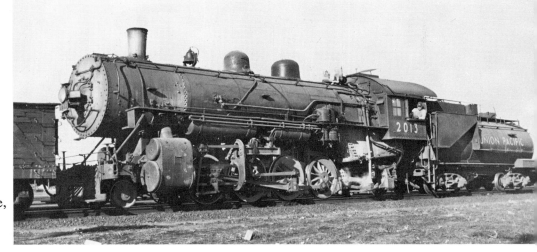

2013, ex-OSL Mike, at North Platte, April 9, 1948.—*F. G. Gschwind*

2124, ex-OWRR&N 2-8-2. North Platte, June 4, 1947. 2000 and 2100 series were among the first "off-division" steamers to arrive after the close of World War II.—*F. G. Gschwind*

Most familiar Mikados (or MacArthurs) on the division were the workhorse 2200's. 2238, at Sidney, Nebraska, was typical of the type before headlights were lowered. —*J. F. Larison*

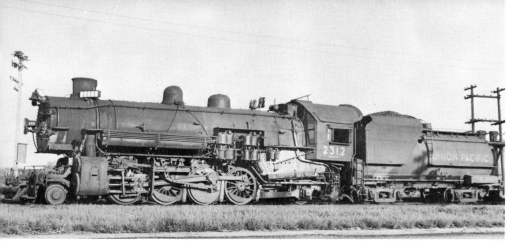

2312 at work on the Third Sub-Division at Sterling, Colorado, August 24, 1953. 2300's were a numerical extension of the 2200 series.—*J. L. Ehernberger Collection.*

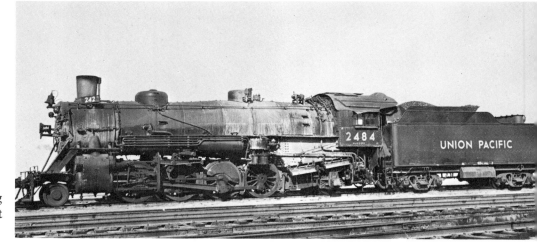

2484 at North Platte in 1955 was among U.S.R.A. power assigned to local freight service.—*F. G. Gschwind*

2557 at Lincoln in February, 1954 was another example of OSL power which became familiar on the division during the final steam years. — *J. L. Ehernberger Collection*

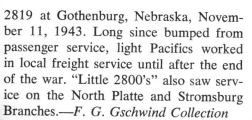

2819 at Gothenburg, Nebraska, November 11, 1943. Long since bumped from passenger service, light Pacifics worked in local freight service until after the end of the war. "Little 2800's" also saw service on the North Platte and Stromsburg Branches.—*F. G. Gschwind Collection*

Speedy 2870 at North Platte on January 28, 1946 was an example of the heavy Pacific on the UP. Last assignments in passenger service on the division were to the "Columbine," an Omaha-Denver local.—*F. G. Gschwind*

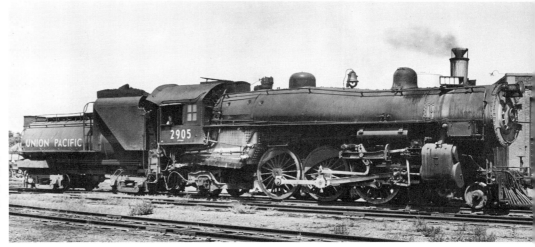

2905 at Sidney, Nebraska, August, 1941, had tender "vestibule" and conical spark arrestor. 2900's saw considerable service on the North Platte branch as well as the main line.—*J. F. Larison*

3224 at Grand Island, 1946, was an oil-burning migrant from OWRR&N.—*J. H. Conant*

3701 4-6-6-4 at North Platte, January 22, 1954. These 3700's were originally in the 3900 series and renumbered when converted to oil burners.—*A. E. Stensvad*

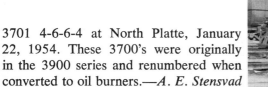

3702 at Sidney, November 19, 1949, was originally the coal-burning 3902, later the oil-fired 3802, became a coal burner again as numbered and finally went back to oil as No. 3802.—*R. H. Kindig*

3801 at North Platte, January 2, 1957. First series Challengers ran their final miles on the Nebraska Division in the early 1950's.—*A. E. Stensvad*

3953 at North Platte, April 13, 1955. Heavy Challengers moved the bulk of tonnage between North Platte and Cheyenne during the final years of steam.— *A. E. Stensvad*

A rare visitor, the 4000, stands beneath the coal chute in North Platte on March 11, 1950. 4-8-8-4's ran east that far, temporarily, during a coal strike. 4013 is in the background and the cab of still another Big Boy is just visible at far right. —*A. E. Stensvad*

A 4400 any way you look at her number, the 4444 at Sidney, August 31, 1955 was typical of standard yard power on the division for years; sister 4466 was one of the last active steamers on the roster.—*F. G. Gschwind Collection*

Oddball 4500 at Grand Island, November, 1945, was rebuilt from 2-8-0 No. 416 in 1924 and was the only 0-8-0 on the system.—*J. H. Conant*

4600, at Beatrice, Nebraska, May, 1955, was a United States Railway Administration 0-6-0 of World War I vintage.—*G. W. Corben Collection*

5021 at North Platte, October, 1949. 2-10-2's were taken for granted and unlauded but worked faithfully and efficiently on the division for decades, despite a lack of fanfare.—*F. G. Gschwind*

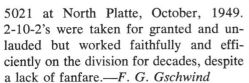

Overland (4-10-2) type 5095 at Grand Island, 1953. Originally three-cylindered engines, numbered in the 8800 series, 5090's came east from southern California.—*J. H. Conant*

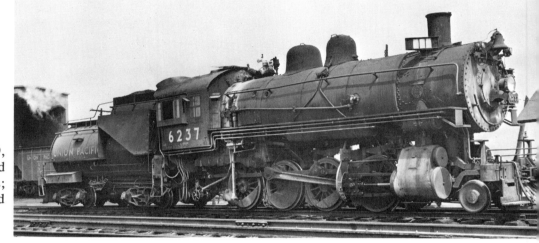

6237 at Hastings, Nebraska, August 19, 1954, was formerly No. 237, renumbered to make way for diesels in the 200 series; had odd rearrangement of bell and sand dome.—*J. L. Ehernberger Collection*

Consolidation 6332 at Valley, Nebraska, September 8, 1957. Like 200's, remaining 300's were renumbered in 1955-56.— *J. L. Ehernberger*

4-8-2's like 7033 at Kearney, November 12, 1954, were once prime passenger power on the Union Pacific but ended their days in freight service. — *F. G. Gschwind*

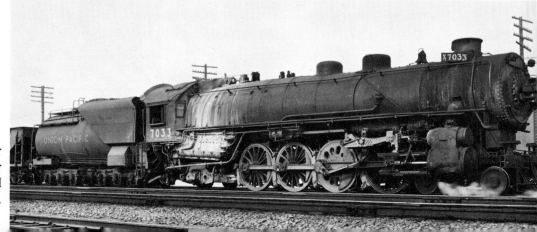

Mountain type 7857 at Yoder, Wyoming, January 26, 1955. 7850 series were originally assigned to LA&SL; were in service on the North Platte Cut-off when steam bowed out there.—*J. L. Ehernbereger*

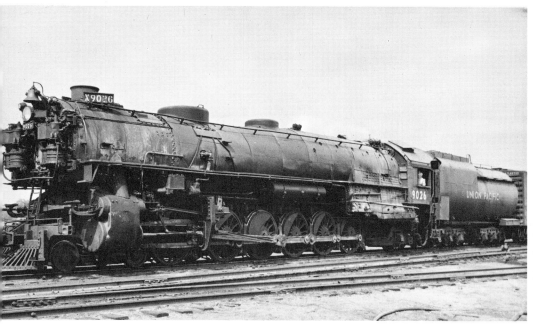

Three-cylindered 4-12-2 (Union Pacific) type was virtually the trademark of the Nebraska Division; the offbeat exhaust was an unforgettable sound. 9026 was photographed at Grand Island, January 2, 1950.—*J. H. Conant*

9505 at North Platte, August 5, 1955. 9500's were virtually identical to 9000's but were assigned to OSL until the late 1940's.—*A. E. Stensvad*

407 stands in the Sidney yards resplendent in new paint as she awaits placement in a park in the western Nebraska city.—*The Photo Center, Sidney*

Not far from the high iron in Lexington stands the 485, a graduate of the Baldwin Locomotive Works, Class of 1903. Motive power undreamed of when she arrived on the system now roars past her resting place each day.—*F. G. Gschwind*

481, fittingly enough, rests in Kearney, from where she made her final trips on the branch to Stapleton in 1955.—*The Kearney Hub*

Far from her old haunts on the Oregon Short Line, the 561 sits out the passing years at Columbus.—*Lou Schmitz*

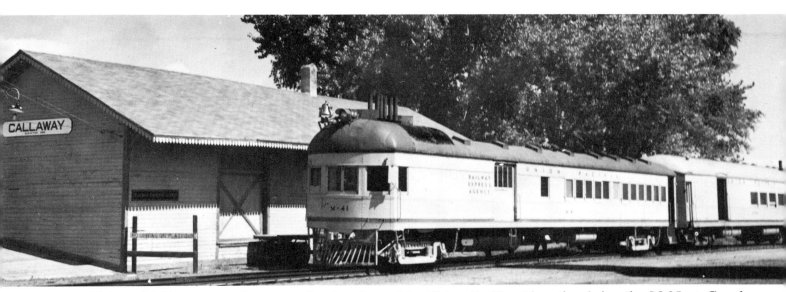

Ill-fated M-41 was one of two gas-electrics donated by Union Pacific, (the other being the M-35 at Grand Island). She poses at Callaway, coupled to the combine of the Kearney Branch local, while deadheading to Stapleton for permanent display. A victim of vandalism, she was scrapped in 1961.—*F. G. Gschwind*

At Hastings, the 6237 and ex-St. Joseph & Grand Island caboose 54 serve as tangible reminders of the Golden Age of Railroading.—*The Hastings Tribune*

Coal cascades into the tender of the 414 via the time-honored bucket system which was still in use at Stapleton on April 7, 1955.—*F. G. Gschwind*

Passenger power lines up under the overpass at North Platte in a nostalgic scene of vanished yesterdays. From left to right in this World War II era scene are the 2905, 2903, 839 and 2872. — *A. E. Stensvad*

9019 is reduced to a stripped-down hulk at the North Platte scrap dock on February 13, 1954.—*A. E. Stensvad*

Snowbound, 1949! Little 117 finds herself no match for the "white hell" which has paralyzed much of the Great Plains in early January of that long and hectic winter. This scene, east of Stapleton, Nebraska, was being repeated over much of the division.—*T. W. Mahoney*

No. 522, a motor train, utilizes Consolidation 430 and a wedge snowplow for breaking through heavy drifts along the branch to Spalding on a wintry day in 1936, as shown here at Cedar Rapids, Nebraska.—*J. H. Conant*

Iron horses in the stable. Challengers rest in their stalls in the North Platte round-house on July 27, 1957.—*A. E. Stensvad*

Drifting steam, caught in the glare of floodlights creates an unusual effect in this nocturnal scene in the Council Bluffs yards as a 4-8-4 and the 9505 simmer in the cool breeze of a September night in 1955.—*W. W. Kratville*

FINALE

The air is clear from horizon to horizon, all along the length of the Nebraska Division. The prairie winds have long since swept away all vestiges of the smoky breath of the Iron Horse. The vast smoke haze which stretched along the Valley of the Platte and hovered over Lodge Pole Creek has vanished forever. The majestic cottonwoods still stand close beside the branch line rails but the hot showers of sparks and cinders no longer rain down upon their foliage. The Union Pacific trains roll on, all along the division, but a page of history has been turned and a chapter closed. Yet the steam locomotive lives on, in memory and in legend, and there remains eternally, in the annals of railroad history, the indelible record of a Golden Age when there was Smoke Across the Prairie.

NEBRASKA DIVISION
FIRST SUBDIVISION
MAIN LINE—COUNCIL BLUFFS TO GRAND ISLAND

Sta. No.	Dist. from Co. Bluffs	STATION	Tel. Call	Kind of Agency	Class of Frt. Sta.	Location of Frt. Platform from Co. B.	Stock Yard Facilities
......	0.0	Co. Bluffs Union Depot......Iowa	......	T			
......		Co. Bluffs, 10th Ave. do	......	F	A		Yes
0		Co. Bluffs Transfer. do	......	P	A		
0	2.2	Iowa-Neb. State Line	......				
69	2.4	C. B. & Q. R. R. Crossing......Neb.	......				
......		Omaha City, 1614 Farnam St. do	......	T			
......		Omaha, Gen. Agt. do	......	T			
......		Frt. Dept. do	......	T P			
3	2.8	Omaha, Un.Pass.Sta.do	......	T P			
3	2.8	Omaha, Baggage. do	......				
......		Omaha, Freight, Jones and 9th Sts. do	......	F P	A		
......		Omaha Hdqtrs. Ticket Office.... do	......	T P			
......		Omaha, Headqrts. Tel. do	U	P			
......		Omaha, Supt. Office do	Fr	P			
......		Omaha, Dispatcher do	Rh	P			
......		Omaha, Bdg. Dist. Disp'r. do	Ws	P			
......		Omaha, Store.... do	Yd	P			
......		Omaha, Tel. (Union Sta.) do	Su	P			
5	5.2	Summit (Tower).... do		P			
......	5.5	32nd Avenue do		P			
......	5.6	I. C. R. R. Cross.— M. P. R. R. Cross. do		P			
7	6.9	Foxley.... do		P			
......	8.0	C. & N. W. Ry. Cross. do					
9	8.3	M. P. R. R. Cross. do		P			
14	8.9	Seymour.... do		P	A		
17	13.6	Sarpy.... do		P			
	17.1	Lane.... do	Cj				
5	5.2	Via Old Line—Summit to Lane Summit Tower .... do	Su	P			
......	5.3	C. B. & Q. R. R. Cross.... do					
Z 6	6.4	So. Omaha.... do		F P			
Z 6	6.5	So. Omaha U. S. Yds. do		F T P	A		Yes
Z 10	10.2	Avery.... do		P		L	Yes
......	10.9	Gilmore Tower.... do	Jn	P		L	
Z 12	11.9	Gilmore.... do		P	A	L	Yes
......	13.4	C. R. I. & P. Ry. Cross.... do					
Z 17	16.8	Papillion.... do	Po	F X P	A	L	Yes
Z 19	19.2	Portal—M. P. R. R. Cross.... do					
......	20.0	C. B. & Q. R. R. Cross.... do					
Z 23	22.5	Millard.... do	Md	F X P	A	L	Yes
17	26.1	Lane.... do	Cj				
22	21.7	Elkhorn.... do	Kh	F T X P	A	L-O	Yes
25	24.5	Waterloo.... do	Wo	F T X P	A	R	Yes
28	28.0	Valley.... do	V	F T X P	A	L-S	Yes
34	34.3	Mercer.... do		P	A		
......	38.2	F. S. Y. & L. Co. Cross.... do					
......	39.3	Fremont, Un. Pass. Sta.... do	Fn	T P	A	R-OE	
39		Fremont, Freight, do		F P			
......	40.0	C. B. & Q. R. R. Cross.... do		P			

Note—For accounting purposes the Iowa-Nebraska state line is assumed to be and remain at the middle of the bridge 2.25 miles from Council Bluffs.

NEBRASKA DIVISION
FIRST SUBDIVISION—Concluded
MAIN LINE—COUNCIL BLUFFS TO GRAND ISLAND—Concluded

Sta. No.	Dist. from Co. Bluffs	STATION	Tel. Call	Kind of Agency	Class of Frt. Sta.	Location of Frt. Platform from Co. B.	Stock Yard Facilities
......	44.8	(C.&N.W.Ry.Cross.Neb.)		P			
46	46.3	Ames.... do	Nb	F T X P	A	R	Yes
54	54.4	North Bend.... do	Dj	F T X P	A	R	Yes
61	61.4	Rogers.... do	Sc	F T X P	A	L-O	Yes
69	68.7	Schuyler.... do	Bs	F T X P	A	L	
77	76.9	Richland.... do					
......	83.8	C. B. & Q. R. R. Cross.... do		P			
85	84.5	Columbus, Pass.... do	C	T P			
......		Columbus, Baggage.... do		X P			
......		Columbus, Frt.... do		F P	A	RL-SE	Yes
92	92.2	Duncan.... do	Dq	F T X P	A	L-S	Yes
97	96.5	Gardiner.... do		P	A		
102	102.3	Silver Creek.... do	Si	F T X P	A	L	Yes
108	107.9	Havens.... do		P	A		
113	113.0	Gibson,Stock Yards do			A		
114	113.6	Clarks.... do	Cz	F T X P	A	R	Yes
119	119.1	Thummel.... do		P	A		
124	123.8	Stock Yards.... do			A		
......	124.3	C. B. & Q. R. R. Cross.... do					
125	124.9	Central City.... do	Ci	F T P	A	L-E	Yes
129	128.5	Paddock.... do		P	A		
135	135.1	Chapman.... do	Cp	F T X P	A	L	Yes
141	140.7	Lockwood.... do		P	A		
......	146.5	C. B. & Q. R. R. Cross.... do		P			
147	146.9	Grand Island, Pass.... do		T P			
......		Grand Island, Frt.... do		F P	A	RL-SE	
......		Grand Island, Bge.... do		X P			
......		Grand Island, Tele.... do	Ge	P			
......		Grand Island,Disp'r do		P			
......		Grand Island, Yard Tel.... do	Gd	P			

BEATRICE BRANCH

Sta. No.	Dist. from Valley	STATION	Tel. Call	Kind of Agency	Class of Frt. Sta.	Location of Frt. Platform from Co. B.	Stock Yard Facilities
28	0.0	Valley......Neb.	V	F T X P	A	L-S	Yes
......	0.1	Valley (Jct. H. B.) do					
......	0.9	Consumers Sand Co. Spur do		A			
......	1.7	Davis-Hadden Spur.... do		A			
......	5.8	C. B. & Q. R. R. Cross.... do					
UA 6	6.3	Yutan.... do	Yn	F X P	A	R	
UA 12	11.6	Mead.... do	Ad	F X P	A	L-S	Yes
UA 19	18.9	Wahoo.... do	W	F P	A	R-S	Yes
......	19.6	C. & N. W. Ry. Cross.... do					
......	19.6	C. B. & Q. R. R. Cross.... do					
UA 26	26.3	Weston.... do	Wn	F X P	A	R	
UA 33	33.2	Touhy.... do		P	A		
UA 37	37.3	Valparaiso.... do	Vo	F T X P	A	R	Yes
UA 42	41.8	Agnew.... do		P	A		
UA 47	46.5	Raymond.... do	Rm	F T X P	A	L	Yes
UA 53	52.7	Garratt.... do		P	A		
UA 55	55.3	West Lincoln.... do			A		
......	55.5	C. B. & Q. R. R. Cross.... do					
......		Lincoln City, 130 So. 13th St.... do		T			
UA 57	57.2	Lincoln, Pass.... do	Ni	T			
UA 57	57.1	Lincoln, Frt.... do	Sn	F P	A	RL-SE	
......		Lincoln, Bge.... do					
......	57.4	C. B. & Q. R. R. Cross.... do					
......	59.0	C. B. & Q. R. R. Cross.... do					
......	62.0	C. R. I. & P. Ry. Cross.... do					
UA 65	65.4	Jamaica.... do		P	A	R	
UA 68	68.2	Hanlon.... do		P	A		
......	69.5	Mo. Pac. R. R. Cross.... do					
UA 75	74.7	Princeton.... do	Rd	P	A		
UA 80	79.5	Cortland.... do	Ft	F T X P	A	L	Yes
UA 89	88.9	Pickrell.... do	Ik	F T X P	A	R	
......	96.0	Kilpatrick Bros. Spur.... do			A		
UA 97	96.8	Beatrice.... do	Bz	F T P	A	R-L	Yes

STROMSBURG BRANCH

Sta. No.	Dist. from Valp.	STATION	Tel. Call	Kind of Agency	Class of Frt. Sta.	Location of Frt. Platform from Co. B.	Stock Yard Facilities
UA 37	0.1	Valparaiso (Jct. H. B.).Neb.					
UB 7	0.0	Valparaiso.... do	Vo	F T X P	A	R	Yes
UB 14	7.4	Loma.... do			A		
......	13.5	Brainard.... do	Bd	F T X	A	R-O	
......	15.0	C. & N. W. Ry. Cross.... do					
UB 23	22.7	Power House Spur.... do			A		
......	23.2	David City.... do	Dv	F T X	A	L-O	
UB 28	23.5	C. B. & Q. R. R. Cross.... do			A		
UB 33	27.9	Foley.... do			A		
UB 40	33.3	Rising City.... do	Rn	F T X	A	R	
UB 48	40.1	Shelby.... do	Sh	F T X	A	R-S	
UB 53	47.5	Osceola.... do	Oz	F T X	A	L-S	
UB 57	52.9	Stromsburg.... do		F T X	A		
UB 63	56.8	Durant.... do			A	L	
UB 69	63.0	Polk.... do	Pk	F T X	A	R	Yes
......	68.5	Hordville.... do	Hv	F T X	A		
UB 74	73.3	Sand Spur.... do			A		
......	73.8	Heber.... do			A		
......	75.3	C. B. & Q. R. R. Cross.... do		P			
125	75.9	Central City.... do	Ci	F T P	A	L	

NORFOLK BRANCH

Sta. No.	Dist. from Columbus	STATION	Tel. Call	Kind of Agency	Class of Frt. Sta.	Location of Frt. Platform from Co. B.	Stock Yard Facilities
85	0.0	Columbus, Pass.....Neb	C	T P			
......		Columbus, Baggage.... do		X P			
......		Columbus, Frt.... do		F P	A	RL-SE	Yes
......	1.0	Columbus (Jct. H. B.).... do					
UC 4	4.2	Sheldonville.... do			A		
UC 9	9.4	Oconee.... do			A		
UC 15	14.7	Platte Center.... do	Pc	F T X P	A	R	
UC 20	20.3	Tarnov.... do			A		
......	25.1	C. & N. W. Ry. Cross.... do					
UC 26	25.7	Humphrey.... do	Hj	F T X	A	R-O	Yes
UC 29	29.1	Peck.... do		P	A		
UC 35	35.4	Madison.... do	Ma	F T X	A	R-SE	Yes
UC 41	40.9	Enola.... do			A		Yes
......	48.7	C. & N. W. Ry. Cross.... do					
......	50.2	Creighton Branch, C. & N. W. Ry. Cross. do					
UC 50	50.4	Norfolk.... do	Kn	F T P	A	R-E	Yes

ALBION BRANCH

Sta. No.	Dist. from Oconee	STATION	Tel. Call	Kind of Agency	Class of Frt. Sta.	Location of Frt. Platform from Co. B.	Stock Yard Facilities
UC 9	0.0	Oconee.....Neb.		P	A		
......	0.1	Oconee (Jct. H. B.).... do					
UD 4	4.3	Monroe.... do	Mn	F T X	A	R	
UD 11	11.3	Genoa.... do	G	F T X P	A	RL	Yes
UD 19	18.8	Woodville.... do			A		Yes
UD 22	22.3	St. Edward.... do	St	F T X	A	R-O	Yes
UD 27	27.3	Boone.... do			A		Yes
UD 34	33.7	Albion.... do	A	F T X	A	RL	Yes

CEDAR RAPIDS BRANCH

Sta. No.	Dist. from Genoa	STATION	Tel. Call	Kind of Agency	Class of Frt. Sta.	Location of Frt. Platform from Co. B.	Stock Yard Facilities
UD 11	0.0	Genoa.....Neb.	G	F T X P	A	RL	Yes
......	0.1	Genoa (Jct. H. B.).... do					
UE 5	5.3	Merchiston.... do			A		Yes
UE 9	9.4	Fullerton.... do	Fu	F T X	A	R	Yes
UE 14	13.7	Belgrade.... do		F T X	A	R-O	Yes
UE 22	22.2	Stock Yard Siding.... do			A		Yes
UE 23	23.1	Belgrade.... do	Bl	F T X	A	L	Yes
......	29.9	Mill Spur.... do			A		Yes
UE 30	30.3	Cedar Rapids.... do	Cd	F T X	A	R	Yes
UE 37	36.6	Primrose.... do		F T X	A	R	Yes
UE 44	44.3	Spalding.... do	Sg	F T X	A	RL-S	Yes

ORD BRANCH

Sta. No.	Dist. from Grd. Isld.	STATION	Tel. Call	Kind of Agency	Class of Frt. Sta.	Location of Frt. Platform from Co. B.	Stock Yard Facilities
147	0.0	Grand Island, Pass.....Neb.		T P			Yes
......		Grand Island, Frt.... do		F P	A	RL-SE	
......		Grand Island, Bge.... do		X P			
......		Grand Island, Tele.... do	Ge	P			
......		Grand Island, Dispr.... do	H	P			
......		Grand Island, Yard Tele. do	Gd	P			
......	0.4	C. B. & Q. R. R. Cross.... do					
......	0.5	Grand Island (Jct. H. B.).. do					
UF 3	2.5	Carey.... do			A		
UF 11	11.1	St. Libory.... do	Ry	F T X	A	R	Yes
UF 22	21.9	St. Paul.... do	Sp	F T X	A	L-O	Yes
......	22.2	C. B. & Q. R. R. Cross.... do					
UF 31	30.7	Elba.... do	Eb	F T X	A	L-S	Yes
UF 37	36.8	Cotesfield.... do			A	R	Yes
UF 43	43.1	Week's Spur.... do			A		Yes
UF 45	44.5	Scotia Junction.... do			A		
UF 46	45.7	Scotia (Scotia Branch).... do	Sk	F T X	A	L-O	
UF 49	48.8	North Loup.... do	Nu	F T X	A	L-S	Yes
UF 58	58.4	Saunders.... do			A		
......	60.7	C. B. & Q. R. R. Cross.... do					
UF 61	61.0	Ord.... do	Rd	F T X	A	L-O	Yes

LOUP CITY BRANCH

Sta. No.	Dist. from St. Paul	STATION	Tel. Call	Kind of Agency	Class of Frt. Sta.	Location of Frt. Platform from Co. B.	Stock Yard Facilities
UF 22	0.0	St. Paul.....Neb.	Sp	F T X	A	L-O	Yes
UG 8	8.3	Dannebrog.... do	Db	F T X	A	R	Yes
UG 19	18.6	Boelus.... do	Hw	F T X	A	R	Yes
UG 26	25.8	Rockville.... do	Rv	F T X	A	R	Yes
UG 39	39.0	Loup City.... do	Op	F T X	A	R-O	Yes

PLEASANTON BRANCH

Sta. No.	Dist. from Boelus	STATION	Tel. Call	Kind of Agency	Class of Frt. Sta.	Location of Frt. Platform from Co. B.	Stock Yard Facilities
UG 19	0.0	Boelus.....Neb.	Hw	F T X	A	R	Yes
......	0.3	Boelus (Jct. H. B.).... do					
......	8.8	C. B. & Q. R. R. Cross.... do					
UH 12	12.4	South Ravenna.... do			A	L	Yes
UH 16	15.5	Poole.... do			A	R	Yes
UH 22	22.1	Pleasanton.... do	Pn	F T X	A	L	Yes

SECOND SUBDIVISION
MAIN LINE—GRAND ISLAND TO NORTH PLATTE

Sta. No.	Dist. from Co. Bluffs	STATION	Tel. Call	Kind of Agency	Class of Frt. Sta.	Location of Frt. Platform from Co. B.	Stock Yard Facilities
147	146.9	Grand Island, Pass.Neb.		T P			Yes
......		Grand Island, Frt.... do		F P	A	RL-SE	Yes
......		Grand Island, Bge.... do		X P			
......		Grand Island, Tele. do	Ge	P			
......		Grand Island, Disp. do	H	P			
......		Grand Island, Yard Tel. do	Gd	P			
......	148.5	Sugar Factory Spur do		P	A		
......	149.0	Stock Yards Sdg.... do		P	A		
155	154.5	Alda.... do	Da	F T X P	A	R-SE	Yes
162	162.3	Wood River.... do	Wr	F T X P	A	L-S	Yes
170	169.9	Shelton.... do	St	F T X P	A	L-S	Yes
176	176.0	Gibbon.... do	Gb	F T X P	A	R	Yes
180	180.2	Optic.... do		P	A		
184	184.3	Buda.... do		P	A	L-SE	
189	189.1	Kearney, Pass.... do	Kr	T P			Yes
......		Kearney, Frt.... do		F P	A	RL-S	Yes
194	194.1	Alfalfa Center.... do		P	A		Yes
198	198.1	Odessa.... do	Dz	F T X P	A	R	Yes
205	204.6	Elm Creek.... do	Qr	F T X P	A	L-O	Yes
213	213.3	Overton.... do	Ov	F T X P	A	L-S	Yes
218	217.9	Josselyn.... do		P	A		
224	224.4	Lexington.... do	Um	F T X P	A	L-S	Yes
233	232.5	Darr.... do		F T X P	A	R	Yes

NEBRASKA DIVISION

SECOND SUBDIVISION—Concluded

MAIN LINE—GRAND ISLAND TO NORTH PLATTE—Concluded

(Automatic Block Signals; Double Track)

Sta. No.	Dist. from Co. Bluffs	STATION		Tel. Call	Kind of Agency	Class of Frt. Sta.	Location of Frt. Platform from Co. B.	Stock Yard Facilities
238	238.2	Cozad	Neb.	Co	F T X P	A	R-O	Yes
243	243.2	Willow Island	do		F T X P	A	L	Yes
249	248.8	Gothenburg	do	Bu	F T X P	A	R-OE	Yes
255	254.5	Vroman	do		P	A		
262	261.5	Brady Island	do	Bi	F T X P	A	L-O	Yes
267	266.6	Hindrey	do		P	A		
271	270.6	Maxwell	do	Mx	F T X P	A	L	Yes
275	274.6	Keith	do			A		Yes
279	278.5	Gannett	do		P	A		
281	280.5	Beck	do			A		
284	284.1	North Platte, Pass.	do		T P			
		North Platte, Frt.	do		F P	A	L-SE	Yes
		North Platte, Bge.	do		X P			
		North Platte, Tele.	do	No	P			
		North Platte, Op'r.	do		P			
		North Platte, Disp.	do	Rn	P			
		North Platte Yard	do	Ny	P			

HASTINGS BRANCH

(Auto. Blk. Sig.)

Sta. No.	Dist. from Gibbon	STATION		Tel. Call	Kind of Agency	Class of Frt. Sta.	Location of Frt. Platform from Co. B.	Stock Yard Facilities
176	0.0	Gibbon	Neb.	Gb	F T X P	A	R	Yes
	1.1	Gibbon (Jct. H. B.)	do		P			
H 283	7.9	Denman	do		P	B	L	Yes
H 275	15.4	Hayland	do	Ha	F X P	A	R	Yes
H 270	20.8	Newmarch	do			A	L	
H 262	28.1	Hastings	do	W	F T P	A		
		Hastings Yard	do	An	P			

Note—Hastings station belongs to Kansas Division.

KEARNEY BRANCH

Sta. No.	Dist. from Kearney	STATION		Tel. Call	Kind of Agency	Class of Frt. Sta.	Location of Frt. Platform from Co. B.	Stock Yard Facilities
189	0.0	Kearney, Pass.	Neb.	Kr	T P			
		Kearney, Frt.	do		F P	A	R	Yes
	0.5	Kearney (Jct. H. B.)	do					
UK 6	5.5	Glenwood Park	do			A		
UK 10	10.1	Riverdale	do		F T X P	A	R	Yes
UK 17	16.8	Amherst	do	Hr	F T X	A	R	Yes
UK 23	22.7	Watertown	do			A	R	
UK 26	26.3	Miller	do	Mr	F T X	A	L	Yes
UK 33	32.5	Sumner	do	Su	F T X	A	L	Yes
UK 40	40.4	Eddyville	do	Vd	F T X	A	R	Yes
UK 46	45.9	Lomax	do			A	L	
UK 52	52.1	Oconto	do	Bs	F T X	A	L	Yes
UK 59	59.1	Lodi	do			A	L	Yes
UK 66	65.5	Callaway	do	Ca	F T X P	A	L	Yes
UK 73	73.1	Milldale	do			A	R	Yes
UK 76	75.8	Finchville	do			A		Yes
UK 83	83.1	Arnold	do	Ad	F T X P	A	L-S	Yes
UK 91	90.6	Logan	do			A		Yes
UK 95	94.6	Hoagland	do			A		Yes
UK 99	99.2	Gandy	do		F T X P	A		Yes
UK102	102.4	Stapleton	do	Sn	F T X	A	R-O	Yes

THIRD SUBDIVISION
MAIN LINE—NORTH PLATTE TO SIDNEY

(Automatic Block Signals; Double Track)

Sta. No.	Dist. from Co. Bluffs	STATION		Tel. Call	Kind of Agency	Class of Frt. Sta.	Location of Frt. Platform from Co. B.	Stock Yard Facilities
284	284.1	North Platte, Pass.	Neb.		T P			
		North Platte, Frt.	do		F P	A	L-S	Yes
		North Platte, Bge.	do		X P			
		North Platte, Tele.	do	No	P			
		No. Platte, Disp'r.	do	Rn	P			
		North Platte Yard	do	Ny	P			
291	290.5	Birdwood	do		P	A	L	Yes
297	296.9	Hershey	do	Of	F T X P	A	R	Yes
301	300.7	O'Fallons	do	Fa	P	A		
302	301.8	Varner	do			A		
303	303.4	Sutherland	do	Su	F T X P	A	R-O	Yes
308	307.9	Dexter	do		P	A		Yes

NEBRASKA DIVISION

THIRD SUBDIVISION—Concluded

MAIN LINE—NORTH PLATTE TO SIDNEY—Concluded

(Automatic Block Signals; Double Track)

Sta. No.	Dist. from Co. Bluffs	STATION		Tel. Call	Kind of Agency	Class of Frt. Sta.	Location of Frt. Platform from Co. B.	Stock Yard Facilities
316	315.5	Paxton	Neb.	Pn	F T X P	A	R-S	Yes
322	321.7	Korty	do		P	A		
328	327.7	Roscoe	do	Ro	F T X P	A	R-S	Yes
335	334.8	Ogallala	do	Gt	F T X P	A	R	Yes
344	343.9	Brule	do	Ru	F T X P	A	R-OE	Yes
349	349.1	Megeath	do			A		Yes
354	353.9	Big Springs	do	Gs	F T X P	A	R-O	Yes
359	359.3	Barton	do		P	A		Yes
363.3	363.3	**Neb.-Colo. State Line**						
365	365.3	Julesburg	Colo.	Jb	F T X P	A	L-O	Yes
371	370.6	Weir	Colo.		P	A		
372.2	372.2	**Colo.-Neb. State Line**						
380	380.3	Chappell	Neb.	Cq	F T X P	A	R-O	Yes
385	385.0	Ottman	do			A		
390	389.7	Lodge Pole	do	Gp	F T X P	A	R-O	Yes
396	396.3	Sunol	do	Un	F T X P	A	L-O	Yes
401	401.0	Colton	do		P	A	L-S	Yes
	406.7	C.B.& Q.R.R.Cross	do					
408	407.5	Sidney, Pass.	do		T P			
		Sidney, Frt.	do		F P	A	R-O	Yes
		Sidney, Tele.	do	Cd	P			

NORTH PLATTE BRANCH

Sta. No.	Dist. from O'Fallons	STATION		Tel. Call	Kind of Agency	Class of Frt. Sta.	Location of Frt. Platform from Co. B.	Stock Yard Facilities
	0.2	O'Fallons (Jct. H. B.)	Neb.					
301	0.0	O'Fallons	do	Fa	P	A		
UL 3	2.8	Coker	do			A		Yes
UL 6	5.9	Glenburnie	do			A	L	
UL 13	12.8	Sarben	do	Ak	F T X P	A	L	Yes
UL 20	19.6	Nevens	do			A	L	Yes
UL 25	24.8	Brogsnville	do			A	R	Yes
UL 28	28.4	Keystone	do	Ks	F T X P	A	L	Yes
UL 31	30.7	Kingsley	do			A		Yes
UL 35	34.9	Martin	do	Sa	F T X P	A	L	Yes
UL 41	41.2	Lemoyne	do		P	A	L	Yes
UL 47	46.8	Belmar	do			A	L	Yes
UL 52	51.7	Ruthton	do			A	L	Yes
UL 59	59.3	Lewellen	do	W	F T X P	A	R-O	Yes
UL 63	63.0	Lutherville	do			A	L	
UL 71	70.8	Oshkosh	do	Ox	F T X P	A	L-O	Yes
UL 82	81.8	Lytle	do			A	R	Yes
UL 86	86.4	Lisco	do	Co	F T X P	A	L-O	Yes
UL 95	95.4	Finley	do			A	R	Yes
UL 100	100.4	Broadwater	do	Br	F T X	A	R	Yes
UL 104	104.2	Riley	do			A		
UL 108	108.4	Kelly	do			A	R	
UL 110	109.6	Towers	do			A		
UL 114	114.1	Northport	do	Np	F T X P	A	R-S	Yes
UL 115	115.3	Burlington Jct	do					
	115.5	C. B. & Q. R. R. Crossing	do					
UL 122	121.8	Mohler	do			A		Yes
UL 127	126.7	South Bayard	do	Cr	F T X P	A		Yes
UL 132	132.1	McGrew	do	Mc	F T X	A	R	Yes
UL 138	137.9	Melbeta	do	Mb	F T X P	A	L	Yes
UL 143	143.3	Brockhoff	do			A		Yes
UL 145	145.0	Gering (Jct. H. B.)	do					
UL 146	145.9	Gering	do	G	F T X P	A	R-S	Yes
UL 151	150.5	Costin	do			A		Yes
UL 152	152.3	Haig	do	Ha	F T X	A	L	Yes
UL 156	155.8	South Mitchell	do	Mi	F T X P	A	L-S	Yes
UL 157	157.1	Pelton	do			A		
UL 160	159.5	Baileyvue	do			A		
UL 162	162.1	South Morrill	do	Bi	F T X P	A	L-O	Yes
UL 164	164.2	Joyce	do			A		

NORTH PLATTE BRANCH—Concluded

Sta. No.	Dist. from O'Fallons	STATION		Tel. Call	Kind of Agency	Class of Frt. Sta.	Location of Frt. Platform from Co. B.	Stock Yard Facilities
UL 167	167.4	Lyman Branch Jct	Neb.					
UL 168	167.9	Lyman	do	Mu	F T X P	A	L-O	Yes
UL168.5	168.5	**Nebraska-Wyoming State Line**						
UL 170	170.1	Canal	Wyo.			A		
UL 173	172.8	Stebbins	do			A		
UL 174	173.7	Huntley	do	Hu	F T X P	A	L	Yes
UL 177	177.0	Holly	do			A		Yes
UL 179	178.9	Bullard	do			A		
UL 182	181.6	Yoder	do	Dr	F T X P	A	L-O	Yes
UP 62	182.1	North Platte Cut-Off Jct.	do					
UL 188	188.1	Veteran	do	Vn	F T X P	A	R-O	Yes
UL 192	191.5	Heldt	do			A		Yes
UL 194	193.6	Buffington	do			A		
UL 196	196.1	Cottier	do		P	A	L	Yes
UL 201	200.6	South Torrington	do	Ri	F T X P	A	R-S	Yes

GERING BRANCH

Sta. No.	Dist. from Gering	STATION		Tel. Call	Kind of Agency	Class of Frt. Sta.	Location of Frt. Platform from Co. B.	Stock Yard Facilities
UL 146	0.0	Gering	Neb.	G	F T X P	A	R-S	Yes
UL 145	0.9	Gering (Jct. H. B.)	do					
UM 5	5.4	Mathers	do			B		Yes
UM 6	6.1	Moon	do			B		
UM 7	7.1	Roubadeau	do			A		
UM 8	8.4	Hilliker	do			B		Yes
UM 10	9.8	Riford	do			B		Yes

LYMAN BRANCH

Sta. No.	Dist. from Lyman	STATION		Tel. Call	Kind of Agency	Class of Frt. Sta.	Location of Frt. Platform from Co. B.	Stock Yard Facilities
UL 168	0.0	Lyman	Neb.	Mu	FT X P	A	L-O	Yes
	0.4	Lyman (Jct. H. B.)	do					
UN 3	2.8	Sears	do			B		Yes
	3.3	Siding No. 1	do					
UN 5	4.6	Hartman	do			B		Yes
UN 6	6.4	Stegall	do			B		Yes

SEARS BRANCH

Sta. No.	Dist. from Sears	STATION		Tel. Call	Kind of Agency	Class of Frt. Sta.	Location of Frt. Platform from Co. B.	Stock Yard Facilities
UN 3	0.0	Sears	Neb.			B		Yes
UO 1	1.2	Bellinger	do			B		
UO 3	2.8	Janise	do			B		Yes

FOURTH SUBDIVISION

MAIN LINE—SIDNEY TO CHEYENNE

(Automatic Block Signals; Double Track)

Sta. No.	Dist. from Co. Bluffs	STATION		Tel. Call	Kind of Agency	Class of Frt. Sta.	Location of Frt. Platform from Co. B.	Stock Yard Facilities
408	407.5	Sidney, Pass.	Neb.		T P			
		Sidney, Frt.	do		F P	A	R-O	Yes
		Sidney, Tele.	do	Cd	P			
416	415.5	Brownson	do	Bw	P	A	L-OE	Yes
426	426.4	Potter	do	Pr	F T X P	A	R-O	Yes
431	430.9	Jacinto	do			A		
435	435.4	Dix	do	Dx	F T X P	A	L-S	Yes
440	439.9	Owasco	do		P	A	R	Yes
445	444.5	Kimball	do	Kb	F T X P	A	L-SOE	Yes
451	451.1	Oliver	do			A		
457	456.6	Bushnell	do	Bn	F T X P	A	L-O	Yes
461	460.9	Smeed	do			A	L	
465.7	465.7	**Neb.-Wyo. State Line**						
467	466.7	Pine Bluffs	Wyo.	Uf	F T X P	A	L-S	Yes
472	472.0	Tracy	do			A		
478	477.5	Egbert	do	Gx	F T X P	A	R	Yes
483	483.2	Burns	do	Ux	F T X P	A	L	Yes
490	489.7	Hillsdale	do	Hd	P	A	R	Yes
496	495.9	Durham	do		P	A	L	
501	501.2	Archer	do	Rd	P	A	L	Yes
	506.3	C. B. & Q. R. R. Crs	do					
		Cheyenne City, 120. W. 16th St.	do		T P			
510	509.5	Cheyenne, Pass.	do		T			
		Cheyenne, Frt.	do		F	A	R-SE	Yes
		Cheyenne, Bge.	do		P			
		Cheyenne, Tele.	do	N	P			
		Cheyenne, Yard Telegraph Office	do	Cy	P			
		Cheyenne, Disp'r.	do	Di	P			

Note—Cheyenne belongs to Wyoming Division.

NORTH PLATTE CUT-OFF

Sta. No.	Dist. from Egbert	STATION		Tel. Call	Kind of Agency	Class of Frt. Sta.	Location of Frt. Platform from Co. B.	Stock Yard Facilities
	0.2	Egbert (Jct. H. B.)	Wyo.					
478	0.0	Egbert	do	Gx	T X	A	R	Yes
UP 15	14.6	Lindbergh	do	Bg	F T X	A	L	Yes
UP 22	21.8	Albin	do	Ab	F T X	A	L	Yes
UP 34	33.6	Tremain	do			A		Yes
UP 41	40.5	Lagrange	do	Ga	F T X	A	L	Yes
UP 44	43.5	Wycross	do			A		Yes
UP 50	49.6	Duroc	do			A		Yes
UP 52	51.9	Hawk Springs	do	Hk	F T X	A	R	Yes
UP 54	53.8	Creighton	do			B		
UP 57	56.7	Fonda	do			B		Yes
UP 59	58.9	Goodland	do			B		
UP 62	62.1	North Platte Cut-Off Jct.	do					
UL 182	62.7	Yoder	do	Dr	F T X P	A		Yes

EXPLANATION OF LETTERS AND CHARACTERS SHOWN IN LIST OF STATIONS

KIND OF AGENCY—
- F—Freight Station.
- T—Ticket Office.
- X—Express Agency.
- P—Railroad Telephone.
- S—Station operated only certain months of the year.

DISTANCES—
The distances given are measured to and from depots, not to or from initial or junction points of track.

CLASS OF FREIGHT STATION, i. e., amount of freight that may be received or delivered—
- A—Freight will be received or delivered in any quantity.
- B—Carload freight only will be received or delivered.
- C—Less carload freight only will be received or delivered.

LOCATION OF FREIGHT PLATFORM—
- R—Right side of unloading track going from Council Bluffs, Kansas City, Ogden, Granger, Los Angeles, or Portland.
- L—Left side of unloading track going from Council Bluffs, Kansas City, Ogden, Granger, Los Angeles or Portland.

LOCATION OF AUTOMOBILE PLATFORM—
- S—Same side of unloading track as freight platform.
- O—Opposite side of unloading track as compared with location of freight platform.
- E—End of unloading track.
(Combined symbols indicate 2 or more platforms thus,—"SE," same side and end; "OE," opposite side and end; "SOE," both sides and end.)

RATING OF LOCOMOTIVES IN FREIGHT SERVICE, IN TONS OF 2,000 POUNDS

Total weight of trains, exclusive of locomotive and tender, which the different classes of locomotives will haul in each direction between stations named, under favorable weather conditions. A deduction of ten per cent may be made for fast trains.

Type of Locomotive	Numbers (Inclusive)	Council Bluffs to Grand Island	Grand Island to North Platte	North Platte to Sidney	Sidney to Cheyenne	O'Fallons to Gering	Gering to South Torrington	Yoder to Egbert	Valley to Wahoo	Wahoo to Valparaiso	Valparaiso to Lincoln	Lincoln to Beatrice	Hastings to Gibbon	Julesburg to LaSalle
C 57 $\frac{22}{30}$ 190	201 to 358	2300	3150	1500	1200	2250	2550	1300	2680	1200	2680	1800	2680	1700
C 57 $\frac{21}{30}$ 162 172	400 to 498	2000	2870	1300	1000	2000	2500	1200	2440	1100	2440	1400	2440	1500
MacA 57 $\frac{23¾}{30}$ 206 210	1900 to 1949	3400	3490	2000	1600	2500	3150	1500	3300	1540	3300	1900	3000	2100
MacA 63 $\frac{26}{28}$ 212 228	2200 to 2320	3800	3890	2500	1800	2700	3300	1650	3300	1650	3300	2000	3330	2400
MacA 63 $\frac{26}{30}$ 222	2480 to 2499	3800	3970	2500	1800	3000	3360	1750	3300	1650	3300	2000	3400	2500
TTT 63 $\frac{29½}{30}$ 286 311	5000 to 5089	4800	5130	3100	2600				4500	2300	4500	2500	4380	3000
UP 67 $\frac{27}{31\text{-}32}$ 368 372	9000 to 9087	5800	7160	4700	4200				6000	3100	6000	3500	7000	3800
4-6-6-4 3 4 5 69 $\frac{21\text{-}21}{32}$ 406 404 407	3930 to 3949 3950 to 3969 3975 to 3999	5800	7070	4900	4200									4000
4-8-8-4 1 2 68 $\frac{23¾\text{-}23¾}{32}$ 540 545	4000 to 4019 4020 to 4624	6800	8000	6500	6000									
FEF 77 $\frac{24½}{32}$ 266	800 to 819	4540	4540	3100	2600				4250	2300	4250	2500	4380	3200
FEF 80 $\frac{25}{32}$ 266	820 to 844													
P 77 $\frac{25}{26}$ 163 165 167 184 193	2860 to 2899 2900 to 2911 3114 to 3138 3218 to 3227	3400	3400	2000	1400	2800	3000	1200	2500	1350	2500	1900	3000	1700
MT 73 $\frac{29}{28}$ 256 261	7000 to 7038 7850 to 7869	3800	3960	2500	2200	2950	3100	1700	2700	1650	2700	2000	3390	2500

EXPLANATION

C .... Consolidation
MacA .... MacArthur
TTT 2-10-2
UP 4-12-2
FEF 4-8-4
P .... Pacific
MT .... Mountain

EXAMPLE: Consolidation locomotive having 57 inch drivers, cylinders 21 inch diameter and 30 inch stroke, and weighing 162,000 pounds on drivers:

$$\text{C.57} \quad \frac{21}{30} \quad 162$$

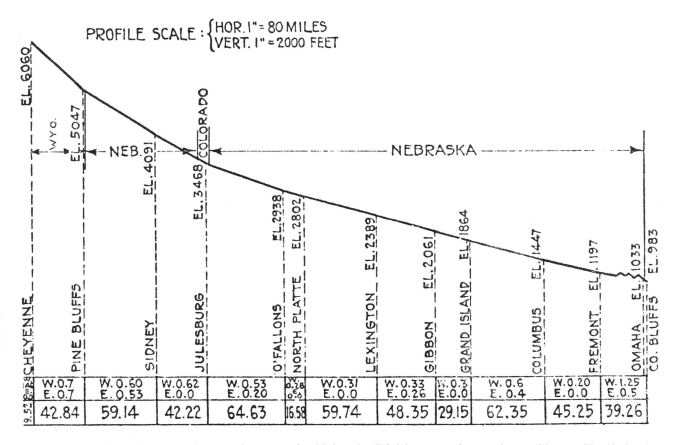

PROFILE SCALE: { HOR. 1" = 80 MILES VERT. 1" = 2000 FEET

CHEYENNE EL. 6060
PINE BLUFFS EL. 5047 (WYO.)
SIDNEY EL. 4091 (NEB.)
JULESBURG EL. 3468 (COLORADO)
O'FALLONS EL. 2938
NORTH PLATTE EL. 2802
LEXINGTON EL. 2389
GIBBON EL. 2061
GRAND ISLAND EL. 1864
COLUMBUS EL. 1447
FREMONT EL. 1197
OMAHA EL. 1033
CO. BLUFFS EL. 983

	W. 0.7 E. 0.7	W. 0.60 E. 0.53	W. 0.62 E. 0.0	W. 0.53 E. 0.20	W. 0.28 E. 0.28	W. 0.31 E. 0.0	W. 0.33 E. 0.26	W. 0.3 E. 0.0	W. 0.6 E. 0.4	W. 0.20 E. 0.0	W. 1.25 E. 0.5
9.52	42.84	59.14	42.22	64.63	16.58	59.74	48.35	29.15	62.35	45.25	39.26

Tonnage ratings for steam locomotives, on the Nebraska Division, are shown above. The profile (below), shows ruling grade, both east and westbound, and mileage between major stations.—*Union Pacific R.R.*